IS THERE SEX AFTER 40?

FOR HER

BY TONI GOFFE

"MUM! REALLY! YOU STILL HAVE SEX AT YOUR AGE....? WOW!"

First published in Great Britain by
Pendulum Galley Press
56 Ackender Road, Alton, Hants GU34 1JS

© TONI GOFFE 1992

**IS THERE SEX AFTER 40 FOR HER?
ISBN 0-948912-20-0**

PRINTED 1992

All rights reserved. No part of this publication may be reproduced or transmitted in any form or by any means, electronic or mechanical, including photocopying, recording, or any information storage and retrieval system, or for a source of ideas without permission in writing from the publisher.

Printed in Britain by Abbeyfield Press Northampton

'WHERE DID YOU COME FROM? I'M NOT DOING THE SCHOOL-RUN TILL NEXT WEEK!...

'WELL, YOU TRY FITTING AN AFFAIR IN BETWEEN SHOPPING AND THE VETS...'

'YES, WE'RE SEPARATED, BUT HE KEEPS COMING BACK TO APOLOGISE...'

'A FINE FIGURE OF TWO MEN, I'D SAY...'

These are just some of the books in this series. Why not start a collection? If you can't find them contact us.

CAN SEX IMPROVE YOUR GOLF? Do you get ball compression in the sweet spot? Do you keep losing your grip? What does fore-play have to do with golf? and can sex improve it? Don't 'play around' till you've read this book.

FARTING. All you want to know about 'blowing off' but were afraid to ask. The history of farting; the what, why, where and when of Farting; having fun with Farting and famous Farts including the 'silent-but-deadly' Fart. Don't miss this one.

IS THERE SEX AFTER 40? Now in a two book form. 'FOR HIM' and 'FOR HER'. Can one still get one's leg over at this great age? What do you do with the kids? Can you fit an affair in between shopping and the vet's? Why not get both books?

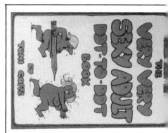

THE VERY, VERY, SEXY ADULT DOT-DOT BOOK. Draw your own very, very, sexy cartoon. That's if your hand isn't shaking too much. Read the very, very, sexy caption your own cartoon, you'll need a mirror for this. While you've got the mirror, why don't you . . . .

ARE YOU STILL FLIRTY AT 30? Is there time for sex between collecting the kids and meeting your husband's train, and getting the film developed? Are you getting enough sexual harassment in the office? What you need is a nice sex cocktail.

ARE YOU FINISHED AT 50? Is it harder to get the old leg over these days? Harder to blow out your birthday candles? What about chasing your secretary around your desk? Do you need 5 minutes start? You're only finished when you're finished. Right?

THE NEW SEX DIET. How to lose weight everybody's favorite way. Sex causes friction. Friction causes burning. Burning causes calorie loss. Calorie loss means weight loss. So lose weight with lots and lots of SEX. The more you do it the more you lose. So get going.

HAPPY? BIRTHDAY. When you blow out the candles on your birthday cake --- is this a blow job? Watch out for the birthday blackmail-o-gram . . . . . . Anyway happy birthday bumping **Keep an eye open for the kids with the video.**

PENDULUM GALLERY PRESS   56 Ackender Road, Alton, Hampshire. GU34 1JS   Tel: (0420) 84483